The Problem-Solving Workbook

by Tracy Zimmerman
Illustrated by Steve Barr

Childswork ChildsPLAY

Plainview. New York

The Problem-Solving Workbook
by Tracy Zimmerman
Illustrated by Steve Barr

Childswork/Childsplay publishes products for mental heath professionals, teachers and parents who wish to help children with their developmental, social and emotional growth. For questions, comments, or to request a free catalog describing hundreds of games, toys, books, and other counseling tools, call 1-800-962-1141.

Childswork/Childsplay grants limited permission for the copying of this publication for individual professional use. For any other use, no part of this book may be reproduced or transmitted in any form or by any means, electronic or mechanical, including photocopying, recording, or by any information storage and retrieval system, without written permission from the publisher.

INTRODUCTION FOR ADULTS

The Problem-Solving Workbook is designed to teach children a six-step problem-solving process by putting them into the role of a detective. The book is designed for children aged 7 through 12. Adult guidance may be necessary with younger children to help them learn the problem-solving process.

Adults may also wish to use this book with older children who have behavioral problems, to guide them through the problem-solving process and to give them more direct and immediate feedback about their answers.

Teachers and counselors might prefer to use this book in group discussions with children. The teacher or counselor could lead the children in a discussion of each case, and then write down the answers that the group decides upon.

Once this problem-solving process has been learned, it may be useful in helping children solve their own problems in school, at home, or with their friends. When children have problems, as shown by their behaviors or by their distressed emotional state, you may want to remind them that they can think their problems through, much like they did using this workbook.

INTRODUCTION FOR CHILDREN

Have you ever wanted to be a detective like Sherlock Holmes or one of the police detectives who you see on TV? Detectives solve problems by thinking things through. First they gather the facts, then they analyze them, then they think of different possible solutions (these are called "alternatives"), and then they decide on the best solution.

When a detective has decided on the best solution, he or she acts on it. Sometimes the detective makes an arrest. Sometimes he or she finds another way to solve the problem. But did you know that sometimes detectives are wrong? Sometimes they think that they have solved the problem, but when they go to act on the solution, they see that they have made a mistake. This happens all the time in life.

Sometimes we come up with a great solution, but it doesn't really work as well as we think. So what do you do? Give up? Of course not! A good detective never gives up. You use the new facts you have learned and come up with a new solution.

There are 40 cases for you to solve in this workbook. When you complete the workbook and solve all of the cases, you will be a Master Detective. There is a certificate on the last page of this workbook which you can cut out, fill in, and hang up in your room (or your own detective agency).

But first you need to pass your Junior Detective Test. To pass the test, you must remember all five Problem-Solving Steps, and you must solve the practice case.

The five problem-solving steps are:

1. Identify the problem.
2. Gather the facts.
3. Weigh (compare) alternative solutions.
4. Determine the best solution.
5. Act on the solution and make changes if necessary.

You may find that once you have become a Master Detective, you can use your phenomenal new talents to solve problems in your own life.

Maybe sometimes your parents yell at you. You'll be able to know what to do about it!
Maybe your grades aren't as good as you want them to be. You'll find a way to make them better!
Maybe there are kids at school who pick on you. You'll know just what to do, to make things easier for you.

Table of Contents

Take Test Case #1. This is the same format that you will use in solving the other cases in this book. Then check your answers against the ones given by the President of the **"I'VE GOT THE ANSWER" DETECTIVE AGENCY, INC., Master Detective Mr. Imaso Smart.**

TEST CASE #1: THE CASE OF THE MISSING GLOVES

Janine's mom made her wear her blue gloves because the weatherman said that it would be just 20 degrees. Janine got on the bus, pushed past Billy who was blocking the aisle and grabbing at everyone, and sat down next to her best friend Ruth. They talked the whole way to school. In fact, they were so busy talking that Janine didn't realize her gloves were no longer in her pockets. When Janine got off the bus at school, she realized that her gloves were missing, and she got back on the bus to look for them. She looked all over the bus, but they weren't there. Later that day, Janine saw Billy's sister at recess wearing blue gloves. What should Janine do?

Solve the problem by filling in the following questions. Then check your answers with the answers provided by Mr. Imaso Smart on page 4. Maybe your answers will be a little different. Sometimes there are different solutions to the same problem. Ask an adult who you think is a good problem-solver to check your answers to the test case. If he or she thinks you did a good job, go on to Case #1.

Always take into consideration the following helpful hints:

- When you gather the facts they must be absolutely true. Facts are not what people think or feel. They are only what actually happened and at least two people must be able to agree that things happened that way. In other words if you see something, but no one else does, then it is not really a fact.

- Many times the best solution will be a combination of one or more alternatives. In deciding upon the best alternative solution, sometimes it is helpful to get other people's opinions.

- When solving the other cases in this workbook, imagine what you think would happen when you act on a solution. Close a case when everyone is satisfied with the solution.

The Problem: _____

_____

The Facts: _____

_____

_____

_____

Weigh the alternatives:	What makes you think this is a good solution (the pluses)?	What would happen if your solution was wrong (the minuses)?
Alternative A		
Alternative B		
Alternative C		

Write down the best solution you can. _____

_____

_____

_____

Act on the solution and make changes in the solution if necessary. _____

_____

_____

_____

The Problem: Janine doesn't have her gloves, and must either find them or have a good explanation for her mother.

The Facts:

Fact 1: Janine had the gloves when she got on the bus.

Fact 2: Janine did not have them when she got off the bus.

Fact 3: Billy was acting silly on the bus, pushing and shoving.

Fact 4: Billy's sister was wearing similar gloves later that day.

Weigh the alternatives:	What makes you think this is a good solution (the pluses)?	What would happen if your solution was wrong (the minuses)?
Alternative A Janine should accuse Billy's sister of taking her gloves	It seems logical, and Billy might admit he took them and give them back.	If Janine is wrong, she will have done something very unfair.
Alternative B Janine should ask Billy's sister if she has seen the gloves that she lost.	Billy's sister might say "yes" and give them back.	Nothing bad would happen, even if Billy's sister said "no."
Alternative C Janine should forget about Billy's sister and keep looking for the gloves. She should go to the school Lost & Found and ask if the gloves have turned up. Janine should be honest in explaining to her mother what happened.	In this solution, Janine takes responsibility for what happened and deals with the situation openly and honestly.	There is always a chance that Janine will be punished for losing her gloves, even though she didn't really "lose" them and they were stolen.

Write down the best solution you can. Janine should combine alternatives "B" and "C." She should should ask Billy's sister if she has seen her gloves. She should also go to the Lost & Found and ask if anyone has seen her gloves. If the gloves don't turn up, then Janine should tell her mother everything that happened, including how she tried to solve the problem herself. Janine should not blame other people, but should think of ways that she can keep track of her gloves.

Act on the solution and make changes in the solution if necessary. Janine talked to Billy's sister and Janine got a closer look at the gloves. She could see that they had a red stripe on the bottom and were not hers. Janine's gloves never turned up, but Janine told the story to her mother, who was very understanding. Janine had a second pair of gloves which her mother pinned to the sleeves of her coat.

5

CASE #1: THE CASE OF THE UNWANTED FRIEND

Whenever Amy plays in her backyard, Jill wants to come over and play with her. Amy doesn't really like Jill, but she lives next door, and Jill always seems to be around.

To make things worse, Jill likes to take out all Amy's dolls and games and she makes a big mess. It seems like whenever Jill comes over Amy's Dad comes home early and yells at Amy because the whole house is a mess.

The Problem: _____

_____

The Facts: _____

_____

_____

_____

_____

Weigh the alternatives:	What makes you think this is a good solution (the pluses)?	What would happen if your solution was wrong (the minuses)?
<u>Alternative A</u>		
<u>Alternative B</u>		
<u>Alternative C</u>		

Write down the best solution you can. _____

_____

_____

_____

Act on the solution and make changes in the solution if necessary. _____

_____

_____

CASE #2: THE CASE OF THE FUNNY STUDENT

Bill is really funny during class. He calls out and makes smart remarks back to the teacher and makes everyone laugh. Everybody, that is, except the teacher. She gets mad at Bill nearly every day, and sends him to detention when all the other children go home for the day.

The weird part is, Bill isn't really sure why he does what he does. All the kids think he's funny and they all like him, but he keeps getting in trouble. To make things worse, Bill's baseball coach says that he is going to get thrown off the team, because he is missing too many practices by being in detention.

When Bill tries to be more serious in class and tries to answer questions, the other kids make faces at him and try to get him to do something silly. Bill wants to learn and stay out of trouble, but he doesn't know how.

The Problem: _____

_____

The Facts: _____

_____

_____

_____

Weigh the alternatives:	What makes you think this is a good solution (the pluses)?	What would happen if your solution was wrong (the minuses)?
Alternative A		
Alternative B		
Alternative C		

Write down the best solution you can. _____

_____

_____

Act on the solution and make changes in the solution if necessary. _____

_____

_____

CASE #3: THE CASE OF THE EMBARRASSED SON

Matthew's mom drinks a lot. Sometimes when he gets home from school he finds her home from work early, sitting with a can of beer in front of her. His brother Jamie tells him that this is her third beer. He knows his dad will be mad whenever he gets home, which some nights isn't until 9 p.m. Then Matthew will have to listen to his parents fight until he goes to bed.

It always seems to get worse when Matthew has his friends over. His mom will try to be like one of them and hang out and eat their pizza and want to play games with them. He thinks it would be okay if she didn't get drunk all the time. Once, his friend Tim asked him if his mom always drank during the week. Matthew was really embarrassed.

The Problem: _____

_____

The Facts: _____

_____

_____

_____

_____

Weigh the alternatives:	What makes you think this is a good solution (the pluses)?	What would happen if your solution was wrong (the minuses)?
Alternative A		
Alternative B		
Alternative C		

Write down the best solution you can. _____

_____

_____

_____

Act on the solution and make changes in the solution if necessary. _____

_____

_____

_____

CASE #4: THE CASE OF THE PICKED-ON KID

Charlie is always getting picked on at school. First it was just the boys pushing him around because he was smaller than they were, but then the girls started in, saying he was annoying and whiny. Charlie talks a lot when he's nervous and he can get on other people's nerves.

Sometimes even the teacher feels like she's had enough with Charlie, and sends him to the principal when he's noisy and disruptive in class. All of this makes Charlie feel even more lonely. He only seems to feel good when he's at home with his brothers, playing video games or playing with his dog. Charlie's parents are worried because he is always alone.

The Problem: _____
_____

The Facts: _____
_____
_____
_____
_____

Weigh the alternatives:	What makes you think this is a good solution (the pluses)?	What would happen if your solution was wrong (the minuses)?
Alternative A		
Alternative B		
Alternative C		

Write down the best solution you can. _____
_____
_____

Act on the solution and make changes in the solution if necessary. _____
_____
_____

CASE #5: THE CASE OF THE BAD UNCLE

Sylvia has a secret that she's not supposed to ever tell anyone. Sometimes when her uncle babysits for her, he wants to play a funny game that Sylvia has never played with anyone before. He touches her private parts and then makes her do the same to him. This makes Sylvia feel really weird and ashamed but she's not sure why. Her uncle tells her it's okay, but that she shouldn't tell anyone about their game. Sylvia has been keeping her secret for a few months now, and the game seems to take longer and longer each time. She feels like she should tell somebody, but who would understand? Didn't her uncle say there was nothing wrong with it?

The Problem: _____

_____

The Facts: _____

_____

_____

_____

Weigh the alternatives:	What makes you think this is a good solution (the pluses)?	What would happen if your solution was wrong (the minuses)?
Alternative A		
Alternative B		
Alternative C		

Write down the best solution you can. _____

_____

_____

_____

Act on the solution and make changes in the solution if necessary. _____

_____

_____

_____

CASE #6: THE CASE OF BASEBALL VS. HOMEWORK

Jeff wants to play baseball with his friends after dinner but after he brought home a "D" on his English test, his mom is making him finish all his homework before he goes anywhere. He's been working hard doing his English homework every night for two weeks. It takes him about two hours, but tonight is his baseball league's play-off game and he doesn't want to miss it.

Jeff's friend Marc is good at English and has offered to bring a copy of his answers so that Jeff can play in the game. This way, Jeff can come home and show his mom his finished homework and play baseball.

The Problem: _____

_____

The Facts: _____

_____

_____

_____

_____

Weigh the alternatives:	What makes you think this is a good solution (the pluses)?	What would happen if your solution was wrong (the minuses)?
Alternative A		
Alternative B		
Alternative C		

Write down the best solution you can. _____

_____

_____

_____

Act on the solution and make changes in the solution if necessary. _____

_____

_____

_____

CASE #7: THE CASE OF THE CONCERNED SISTER

Debbie noticed that when her sister sits down to read, she gets really frustrated and throws her book down and stomps out of the room. When Debbie asks what's the matter, her sister replies, "I hate school. It's too hard for me. I can't understand anything my teacher is talking about."

Debbie has a friend in her class who has a hard time with school, and her friend goes to a special Resource Room for extra help. Debbie wonders whether her sister needs special help, or whether her parents even know that her sister has a problem with school.

The Problem: _____

The Facts: _____
_____
_____
_____
_____

Weigh the alternatives:	What makes you think this is a good solution (the pluses)?	What would happen if your solution was wrong (the minuses)?
Alternative A		
Alternative B		
Alternative C		

Write down the best solution you can. _____
_____
_____
_____

Act on the solution and make changes in the solution if necessary. _____
_____
_____
_____

CASE #8: THE CASE OF THE ABUSIVE DAD

Sometimes when Marla's dad gets really mad, he hits her mom and yells really loudly. It seems like they always argue, but her mom never hits her dad. He's much bigger and meaner, and Marla ends up helping her mom in the end, getting her ice for a swollen eye or a bandage for her cuts. This seems like a lot for a little kid to handle, but Marla is an only child and her mom doesn't seem to have that many friends.

Marla is always the one she asks for help after her dad storms out of the house and drives away to "cool off." Marla's getting worried that her dad might hit her too, but nobody will believe her story because they look like such a nice family and they have a lot of money.

The Problem: _____

_____

The Facts: _____

_____

_____

_____

Weigh the alternatives:	What makes you think this is a good solution (the pluses)?	What would happen if your solution was wrong (the minuses)?
Alternative A		
Alternative B		
Alternative C		

Write down the best solution you can. _____

_____

_____

_____

Act on the solution and make changes in the solution if necessary. _____

_____

_____

CASE #9: THE CASE OF THE FUNNY BUMP

It's been a few weeks since Karl noticed a funny bump under his arm. It hurts a little bit but he hasn't told anyone about it yet because he's afraid he might have to have an operation. He learned in health class last semester about different diseases and how you should always see a doctor if you notice something weird on your body.

Karl's mom doesn't know anything about this, and he knows if he told her, she would take him straight to the doctor. Karl's getting really nervous because the bump is getting bigger and more painful, but he thinks the doctor will hurt him even more.

The Problem: _____

_____

The Facts: _____

_____

_____

_____

Weigh the alternatives:	What makes you think this is a good solution (the pluses)?	What would happen if your solution was wrong (the minuses)?
Alternative A		
Alternative B		
Alternative C		

Write down the best solution you can. _____

_____

_____

Act on the solution and make changes in the solution if necessary. _____

_____

_____

CASE #10: THE CASE OF THE BOY WHO WANTS TO BE OLDER

James thinks he's old enough to walk home from school by himself. His mom was worried that his neighborhood was too dangerous, but he convinced his mom he was ready to do this on his own.

The other day, though, some kids from a gang followed James out of the playground and took his backpack, tossing it over his head, teasing him and pushing him around. He started crying and they called him a baby. They told him that if he told anybody, they would beat him up. James is scared, but he also doesn't want his mom to think he's still a baby.

The Problem: _____

_____

The Facts: _____

_____

_____

_____

_____

Weigh the alternatives:	What makes you think this is a good solution (the pluses)?	What would happen if your solution was wrong (the minuses)?
Alternative A		
Alternative B		
Alternative C		

Write down the best solution you can. _____

_____

_____

_____

Act on the solution and make changes in the solution if necessary. _____

_____

_____

_____

CASE #11: THE CASE OF THE LOST REMOTE

Andy watches TV every afternoon before dinner. Then after dinner, Andy's father sits in his big easy chair and he watches the shows he likes. And every evening, Andy's father looks for the remote control and can't find it. Andy's father yells at his son, tears apart the couch, and searches everywhere in the room. Finally, he finds it and lectures Andy about keep things neat and in their place. Sometimes he sends Andy to his room crying. Once he spanked Andy so hard, Andy couldn't even sit down. But Andy keeps misplacing the remote control.

The Problem: _____

_____

The Facts: _____

_____

_____

_____

_____

Weigh the alternatives:	What makes you think this is a good solution (the pluses)?	What would happen if your solution was wrong (the minuses)?
Alternative A		
Alternative B		
Alternative C		

Write down the best solution you can. _____

_____

_____

_____

Act on the solution and make changes in the solution if necessary. _____

_____

_____

CASE #12: THE CASE OF THE MISSING LUNCH

Gina's mom always packs Gina's favorite lunch: peanut butter and jelly with bananas. Gina's last class before lunch takes her right past her locker, where she puts away her books, picks up her lunch bag, and walks with her friends to the cafeteria.

One day Gina met up with her friends a little later than usual because she had to stop at the office to pick up something her mom left for her. She ran to her locker, picked up her bag, and found her friends in the lunchroom already eating. When she emptied her bag, her sandwich was gone! She was really hungry that day, too. But what upset her most was looking across to the next table and seeing a boy from the next grade eating a peanut butter and jelly sandwich with bananas, and it was wrapped in tin-foil, just like hers.

The Problem: _____

_____

The Facts: _____

_____
_____
_____
_____

Weigh the alternatives:	What makes you think this is a good solution (the pluses)?	What would happen if your solution was wrong (the minuses)?
Alternative A		
Alternative B		
Alternative C		

Write down the best solution you can. _____
_____
_____
_____

Act on the solution and make changes in the solution if necessary. _____
_____
_____
_____

CASE#13 THE CASE OF THE CHEATING STUDENT

There's a strict policy in school about cheating: if you're caught, you get a zero on your test, and if you see someone else cheat, you must report him to the teacher. Since Duane is the smartest kid in class, he doesn't really need to worry about cheating.

Everyone knows how well everybody else does because the teacher makes the students trade papers and grade them all together.

Lately Mark, who usually gets Cs and Ds, has been sitting near Duane whenever there's a test. All of a sudden Mark has started to get As on all of his tests. The teacher is getting kind of suspicious.

The Problem: _____

_____

The Facts: _____

_____

_____

_____

_____

Weigh the alternatives:	What makes you think this is a good solution (the pluses)?	What would happen if your solution was wrong (the minuses)?
Alternative A		
Alternative B		
Alternative C		

Write down the best solution you can. _____

_____

_____

_____

Act on the solution and make changes in the solution if necessary. _____

_____

_____

_____

CASE #14: THE CASE OF THE NEW GIRLFRIEND

Janey's parents are divorced and she spends weekends with her dad. Her mom was really upset when her dad asked for the divorce, and Janey sometimes finds her mom crying in her room all alone. When she asks what's the matter, her mom says that she's lonely and misses Janey's dad.

The last time Janey visited her dad, there was somebody else at his house. He introduced this woman as his new "friend," and the woman tried to be really nice to Janey and even gave her a present. The woman seemed okay, but Janey thought it was weird to see her dad with somebody other than her mom. In the car, when he dropped Janey off at home, her dad told her not to tell her mom about his new girlfriend because it would probably upset her. Janey knows he's right, but it upset her too and she doesn't have anyone one to talk to about it.

The Problem: _____
_____

The Facts: _____
_____
_____
_____
_____

Weigh the alternatives:	What makes you think this is a good solution (the pluses)?	What would happen if your solution was wrong (the minuses)?
Alternative A		
Alternative B		
Alternative C		

Write down the best solution you can. _____
_____
_____
_____

Act on the solution and make changes in the solution if necessary. _____
_____
_____
_____

CASE #15: THE CASE OF SMOKING IN THE GARAGE

One day when Chuck went over to Randy's house to do homework, Randy told him to come out to the garage, saying he had a surprise to show him. When Randy pulled out a pack of cigarettes, Chuck was shocked. They just had a lecture in school about all the bad things that happen to your body when you smoke. What was Randy thinking? Chuck didn't even want to try it, but Randy started making fun of him for being a baby, and Chuck felt kind of stupid and so he tried smoking.

When Chuck got home that night, his mom asked why he smelled like smoke. Chuck thought about how cool he and Randy looked with their cigarettes and thought he might like to try it again, this time in front of some girls. He just said, "I don't know," to his mom's question.

The Problem: _____

The Facts: _____
_____
_____
_____
_____

Weigh the alternatives:	What makes you think this is a good solution (the pluses)?	What would happen if your solution was wrong (the minuses)?
Alternative A		
Alternative B		
Alternative C		

Write down the best solution you can. _____
_____
_____
_____

Act on the solution and make changes in the solution if necessary. _____
_____
_____
_____

CASE #16: THE CASE OF THE FORGETFUL STUDENT

It used to be rare when Marcie left her books or homework at home. She was always prepared for class. But lately Marcie was always forgetful. She left her books at home at least once a week. She misplaced her homework. She lost her knapsack. Her teacher started to worry that something was wrong at home. When her teacher tried to call Marcie's parents, she only got an answering machine, and she never received a call back.

The Problem: _____

_____

The Facts: _____

_____

_____

_____

_____

Weigh the alternatives:	What makes you think this is a good solution (the pluses)?	What would happen if your solution was wrong (the minuses)?
Alternative A		
Alternative B		
Alternative C		

Write down the best solution you can. _____

_____

_____

_____

Act on the solution and make changes in the solution if necessary. _____

_____

_____

CASE #17: THE CASE OF THE FIGHTING FRIENDS

Paula is good friends with Jane and Tammy, but Jane and Tammy don't really like each other. Whenever Paula is playing with Jane and wants to invite Tammy over to join, Jane bad-mouths Tammy, calling her names and saying she's boring. Tammy does the same thing making fun of Jane. But Paula finds good things about both of them and doesn't want to give them up just because they can't get along.

Yesterday Jane told Paula that if she was going to hang around Tammy, she and Paula just couldn't be friends anymore. This has really hurt Paula's feelings. Why should she be punished just because they fight so much? She wants to stay friends with them both but she doesn't know how.

The Problem: _____

The Facts: _____
_____
_____
_____

Weigh the alternatives:	What makes you think this is a good solution (the pluses)?	What would happen if your solution was wrong (the minuses)?
Alternative A		
Alternative B		
Alternative C		

Write down the best solution you can. _____
_____
_____

Act on the solution and make changes in the solution if necessary. _____
_____
_____

CASE #18: THE CASE OF THE BIG SECRET

Bill was walking home the back way, over the railroad tracks, even though his mom told him he wasn't allowed to walk that way. He ran into two older boys who were huddled together doing something. Bill minded his own business and kept following the tracks when one of them called out to him to come check out what they had. Bill was a little scared, but he wanted to be cool in front of these boys.

They were smoking marijuana and called him over to see if he wanted any. Bill had never smoked before in his life and didn't want to start now. He just wanted to go home. When he started running away they called him a sissy. When Bill got home his mom wanted to know why he was so late and why he had dust all over his jeans. He didn't know what would make his mom more angry: the fact that he was late, that he had walked by the trains, or that he almost smoked some marijuana.

The Problem: _____

_____

The Facts: _____

_____

_____

_____

Weigh the alternatives:	What makes you think this is a good solution (the pluses)?	What would happen if your solution was wrong (the minuses)?
Alternative A		
Alternative B		
Alternative C		

Write down the best solution you can. _____

_____

_____

_____

Act on the solution and make changes in the solution if necessary. _____

_____

_____

CASE #19: THE CASE OF THE PLAYGROUND BULLIES

Eric and Monica can be pretty mean. They push the littler kids around at the park just because they're the oldest. They always get first choice of swings and can make anybody get off them if they want. They are always team captains for kickball and make fun of the kids who can't kick hard or run fast. Nobody likes them, but if you want to play at this playground you have to listen to Eric and Monica.

The Problem: _____

_____

The Facts: _____

_____

_____

_____

_____

Weigh the alternatives:	What makes you think this is a good solution (the pluses)?	What would happen if your solution was wrong (the minuses)?
Alternative A		
Alternative B		
Alternative C		

Write down the best solution you can. _____

_____

_____

_____

Act on the solution and make changes in the solution if necessary. _____

_____

_____

_____

CASE #20: THE CASE OF THE CANDY BAR SHOPLIFTER

Ever since Sam took a candy bar from the convenience store without getting caught, he's been doing it every day. Sometimes friends will dare him to take more stuff for them while they wait outside. Sam's becoming pretty popular, especially with the older kids, and he likes being known as "dangerous."

Somehow Sam's younger brother found out what he was doing and where he was getting all the candy he ate on the way home. He threatened to tell their parents unless Sam started taking stuff for him. Now Sam feels a little out of control. He thinks it is only a matter of time until he gets caught and isn't sure what to do.

The Problem: _____

_____

The Facts: _____

_____

_____

_____

Weigh the alternatives:	What makes you think this is a good solution (the pluses)?	What would happen if your solution was wrong (the minuses)?
Alternative A		
Alternative B		
Alternative C		

Write down the best solution you can. _____

_____

_____

Act on the solution and make changes in the solution if necessary. _____

_____

_____

CASE #21: THE CASE OF THE NERDY GLASSES

Alice feels like a nerd wearing her new glasses and doesn't want to risk the other kids making fun of her. She knows it's going to be hard doing gymnastics after school wearing them and besides, they give her a headache. None of her friends wear glasses.

When they got home from the eye doctor, Alice's mom told her she knew Alice didn't want to wear them, but that they were very expensive and she needed them to see everything better, including the blackboard. But Alice has been taking them off as soon as she leaves the house, and only puts them on again before she walks in the door in the afternoon. She's really been squinting to see the words on the board and just yesterday her teacher asked her where her new glasses were. Alice knows the teacher will tell her mom she hasn't been wearing them so she tells the teacher that she broke them.

The Problem: _____

The Facts: _____
_____
_____
_____

Weigh the alternatives:	What makes you think this is a good solution (the pluses)?	What would happen if your solution was wrong (the minuses)?
Alternative A		
Alternative B		
Alternative C		

Write down the best solution you can. _____
_____
_____
_____

Act on the solution and make changes in the solution if necessary. _____
_____
_____

CASE #22: THE CASE OF THE RELIGIOUS CONFUSION

Peter's grandma is Catholic but he was raised Jewish. Whenever she watches him for the weekend, she takes him to church even though his parents specifically asked her not to. He learns things there that are very different from what he learns in Hebrew school and it's confusing since he thinks he can't ask questions in either setting. He's heard his parents yelling about his grandma taking him to church and he's scared to tell them that he kind of likes hearing about Jesus and listening to the stories they tell in church. He thinks his parents will be mad at him.

The Problem: _____

_____

The Facts: _____

_____

_____

_____

Weigh the alternatives:	What makes you think this is a good solution (the pluses)?	What would happen if your solution was wrong (the minuses)?
Alternative A		
Alternative B		
Alternative C		

Write down the best solution you can. _____

_____

_____

_____

Act on the solution and make changes in the solution if necessary. _____

_____

_____

CASE #23: THE CASE OF THE WORRIED SISTER

Sally's sister is in high school and has been sneaking out of their room late at night to meet her boyfriend. She climbs out their bedroom window down to his car and doesn't come back until almost 5 a.m. Her sister made Sally swear she wouldn't tell their mom and dad, but Sally's getting worried about her. She hears bad things about her sister's boyfriend and thinks he might hurt her someday if she's not careful. But she always comes home smiling and saying she had a fun time, even though she's really tired and falling asleep in her classes. Sally doesn't think her sister will listen to her and she's getting scared.

The Problem: _____

The Facts: _____
_____
_____
_____
_____

Weigh the alternatives:	What makes you think this is a good solution (the pluses)?	What would happen if your solution was wrong (the minuses)?
Alternative A		
Alternative B		
Alternative C		

Write down the best solution you can. _____
_____
_____
_____

Act on the solution and make changes in the solution if necessary. _____
_____
_____
_____

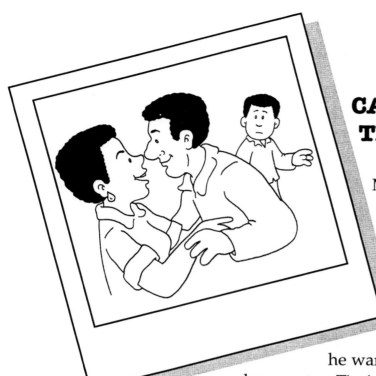

CASE #24: THE CASE OF THE LONELY BOY

Max is considered cool by his friends because his mom doesn't make him do what their moms do. They always complain that they have to be home for supper, can't play outside when it's dark and have to finish all their homework. Max can do whatever he wants, and come home whenever he wants. One thing he often wants to do is hang out at Tim's house. Tim's mom is pretty strict but is really nice and always makes Max do his homework with Tim. She feeds him good dinners too.

The truth is, Max's mom spends all of her time with her new boyfriend. She thinks that Max is happy and so she doesn't worry about him. But sometimes Max comes home from Tim's at 9 p.m. and his mother doesn't even know he was out. Max doesn't know how to talk to her and really doesn't want to talk to her boyfriend. He feels lonely, but he doesn't know why.

The Problem: _____

_____

The Facts: _____

_____

_____

_____

_____

Weigh the alternatives:	What makes you think this is a good solution (the pluses)?	What would happen if your solution was wrong (the minuses)?
Alternative A		
Alternative B		
Alternative C		

Write down the best solution you can. _____

_____

_____

_____

Act on the solution and make changes in the solution if necessary. _____

_____

_____

CASE #25: THE CASE OF THE SNOB

Julianne is really quiet because she's the new girl in her neighborhood. Her mom signed her up for Girl Scouts to help her meet some new friends, but she's too shy to go to any meetings by herself. To everyone in school, Julianne seems like a snob because she doesn't talk to anyone and because she's pretty smart. The other girls have started to ignore her and talk behind her back and they won't let her sit with them at lunch.

Julianne finally found one friend, but she's in an older grade, so she never gets to talk to her that much during school. Julianne doesn't think she's a snob, but she's not sure how to change the other girls' minds.

The Problem: _____

_____

The Facts: _____

_____

_____

_____

_____

Weigh the alternatives:	What makes you think this is a good solution (the pluses)?	What would happen if your solution was wrong (the minuses)?
<u>Alternative A</u>		
<u>Alternative B</u>		
<u>Alternative C</u>		

Write down the best solution you can. _____

_____

_____

_____

Act on the solution and make changes in the solution if necessary. _____

_____

_____

_____

CASE #26: THE CASE OF THE FIGHTING MOTHER AND DAUGHTER

Angela feels strange when her best friend Jane fights with her mom. Sometimes when Angela goes to Jane's house, she'll find Jane screaming at her mom about little things. They seem like little things to Angela, anyway, like putting her favorite shirt in the wash when Jane wanted to wear it to school that day, or making meatloaf for dinner when Jane's mom knows she hates it. Angela just wants to play at Jane's house, but she feels really uncomfortable when Jane's mom keeps interrupting them to fight with Jane.

Angela and Jane are pretty close, and Angela's getting worried about her. Jane's dad left the family four months ago and the fighting seems to have started around then. Jane's no fun to be around because she's always in a bad mood.

The Problem: _____

The Facts: _____

Weigh the alternatives:	What makes you think this is a good solution (the pluses)?	What would happen if your solution was wrong (the minuses)?
Alternative A		
Alternative B		
Alternative C		

Write down the best solution you can. _____

Act on the solution and make changes in the solution if necessary. _____

CASE #27: THE CASE OF THE REAPPEARING DAD

It's been a while since Jackie saw her father. Her parents got divorced when she was only six, and she's now 12 years old. He moved away to another city and started another family. He and his new wife have a baby boy. Jackie's mom has remarried too, and her new husband has a son about Jackie's age.

Just recently, Jackie's dad called her mom saying he would be on vacation in the area and would really like to visit Jackie while he's there. Her mom talked to her about it and said she could make up her own mind. Jackie's been getting used to so many new things, she's not sure she can handle seeing a whole new family and trying to be nice. Her dad is coming this weekend.

The Problem: _____

The Facts: _____
_____
_____
_____
_____

Weigh the alternatives:	What makes you think this is a good solution (the pluses)?	What would happen if your solution was wrong (the minuses)?
Alternative A		
Alternative B		
Alternative C		

Write down the best solution you can. _____
_____
_____
_____

Act on the solution and make changes in the solution if necessary. _____
_____
_____

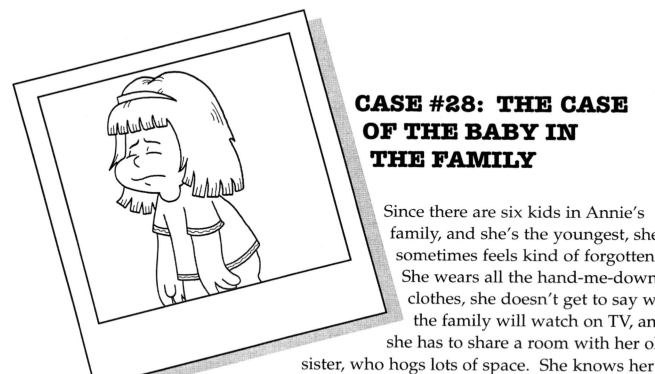

CASE #28: THE CASE OF THE BABY IN THE FAMILY

Since there are six kids in Annie's family, and she's the youngest, she sometimes feels kind of forgotten. She wears all the hand-me-down clothes, she doesn't get to say what the family will watch on TV, and she has to share a room with her older sister, who hogs lots of space. She knows her mom loves her as much as the other kids, but sometimes it seems like she doesn't count as much as everybody else.

Annie's birthday is coming up and she'd really like to have a slumber party. But she knows her oldest brother's graduation is that same weekend. Annie's mom said that there will be lots of relatives who will be visiting, and her party will have to be postponed. Annie understands, but she is really upset.

The Problem: _____
_____

The Facts: _____
_____
_____
_____
_____

Weigh the alternatives:	What makes you think this is a good solution (the pluses)?	What would happen if your solution was wrong (the minuses)?
Alternative A		
Alternative B		
Alternative C		

Write down the best solution you can. _____
_____
_____
_____

Act on the solution and make changes in the solution if necessary. _____
_____
_____

CASE #29: THE CASE OF THE IGNORED BOY

Jason is tired of being ignored at school just because he is short. All the other boys in his fourth grade class are strong and getting tall, and he seems to be taking so long to grow. He gets really upset when he's the last picked for basketball, even after the girls. Sometimes kids make fun of him when he can't make a basket. Once Jason quit in the middle of the game and walked off the court. Then everybody called him a crybaby and it seems that nobody ever forgot about it.

Jason's teacher has pulled him aside to ask what's wrong. He tells her that the other boys are picking on him and won't let him play basketball. The teacher asks Jason how he would like her to help.

The Problem: _____

_____

The Facts: _____

_____

_____

_____

_____

Weigh the alternatives:	What makes you think this is a good solution (the pluses)?	What would happen if your solution was wrong (the minuses)?
Alternative A		
Alternative B		
Alternative C		

Write down the best solution you can. _____

_____

_____

_____

Act on the solution and make changes in the solution if necessary. _____

_____

_____

_____

CASE #30: THE CASE OF THE LAZY BOY

It seems like Mrs. Simmons has it in for James. She always makes him go to the board for the hardest math problems, always calls on him even when other kids are raising their hands, and even makes him stay after school to talk about why he isn't doing so well.

James didn't want to be in this accelerated class in the first place. His teacher and his dad both thought it would be a good idea to stimulate his mind and challenge him. His dad has been so proud of him and brags to all his friends that his son is in the accelerated class. But James would rather take easier classes with the rest of his friends and play baseball after dinner, rather than do extra credit homework. There's probably only about a week left for James to go back to his regular class without missing too much.

The Problem: _____

_____

The Facts: _____

_____

_____

_____

Weigh the alternatives:	What makes you think this is a good solution (the pluses)?	What would happen if your solution was wrong (the minuses)?
Alternative A		
Alternative B		
Alternative C		

Write down the best solution you can. _____

_____

_____

Act on the solution and make changes in the solution if necessary. _____

_____

_____

CASE #31: THE CASE OF THE MEAN GIRL SCOUTS

Lisa is the only African American girl in her Girl Scout Troop. She just joined after her family moved to the neighborhood two months ago. No one has been mean to her, but no one's really that nice either. Her brother is in the Boy Scouts, and all the boys seem to act the same way toward him. They told their mom that they both want to quit because it's no fun. Mom explained that they should give it a chance and try to make friends with the other kids. But Lisa overheard some girls calling her bad names behind her back.

The Problem: _____

The Facts: _____
_____
_____
_____

Weigh the alternatives:	What makes you think this is a good solution (the pluses)?	What would happen if your solution was wrong (the minuses)?
Alternative A		
Alternative B		
Alternative C		

Write down the best solution you can. _____
_____
_____

Act on the solution and make changes in the solution if necessary. _____
_____
_____

CASE # 32: THE CASE OF THE DISAPPEARING APPLE

Carol is always really hungry at lunch time. Her family is kind of poor so her mom can't always afford to pack her a sandwich or fruit. Sometimes she doesn't even get to eat breakfast.

Everybody in the class knows about Carol, so when she asks if she can "borrow" some food, the other kids usually give her something to eat. Every day, though, Susan's apple has been missing from her lunch bag, even though she is one of the people who shares her lunch with Carol. Where could her apples be going? Is her dad forgetting to pack them?

The Problem: _____

_____

The Facts: _____

_____

_____

_____

_____

Weigh the alternatives:	What makes you think this is a good solution (the pluses)?	What would happen if your solution was wrong (the minuses)?
Alternative A		
Alternative B		
Alternative C		

Write down the best solution you can. _____

_____

_____

_____

Act on the solution and make changes in the solution if necessary. _____

_____

_____

CASE #33: THE CASE OF THE EXCLUSIVE CLUB

Julie wants to join the Pep Club at her new school. They organize all the school dances, decorate, and make posters. Julie's really interested in art and thinks this club would be a lot of fun. She notices, however, after signing the waiting list, that it seems that only the most popular girls in the class belong to this club and people who don't have great clothes and live in big houses never seem to get to join.

Julie's dad is one of the teachers at their school. When she doesn't make the cut for new club members, she wants to ask for his help. But part of her also wants to see if she can handle her problem on her own.

The Problem: _____

_____

The Facts: _____

_____

_____

_____

_____

_____

Weigh the alternatives:	What makes you think this is a good solution (the pluses)?	What would happen if your solution was wrong (the minuses)?
Alternative A		
Alternative B		
Alternative C		

Write down the best solution you can. _____

_____

_____

_____

Act on the solution and make changes in the solution if necessary. _____

_____

_____

_____

CASE #34: THE CASE OF THE MISSING MATH BOOK

Luther never loses things. He's a good student and always does his homework. But recently his books and assignments seem to be missing from his desk and his locker. Luther's teacher says that everyone is forgetful sometime, and not to worry about it. But Luther says he is never forgetful. What's going on?

The Problem: _____

_____

The Facts: _____

_____

_____

_____

Weigh the alternatives:	What makes you think this is a good solution (the pluses)?	What would happen if your solution was wrong (the minuses)?
Alternative A		
Alternative B		
Alternative C		

Write down the best solution you can. _____

_____

_____

Act on the solution and make changes in the solution if necessary. _____

_____

_____

CASE #35: THE CASE OF THE STUTTERING STUDENT

When John is called on in class by surprise, he gets really nervous. Even though he studies and usually knows the answers, he doesn't like talking in front of lots of people and he starts to stutter pretty badly. Sometimes it gets so bad that the teacher can't even understand him and he gets so flustered he has to leave the room and get a drink of water to calm down.

The teacher knows John has a speech problem but also knows he has to get over it. When John has a book report to read to the class, his teacher asks him if he wants to stay after school and practice reading it to her. This just makes John mad. He doesn't want to be different from the other kids. He wants to do it on his own, but isn't sure he can get through it.

The Problem: _____

The Facts: _____
_____
_____
_____
_____

Weigh the alternatives:	What makes you think this is a good solution (the pluses)?	What would happen if your solution was wrong (the minuses)?
Alternative A		
Alternative B		
Alternative C		

Write down the best solution you can. _____
_____
_____
_____

Act on the solution and make changes in the solution if necessary. _____
_____
_____

CASE #36: THE CASE OF THE SCARED SWIMMER

Marie is afraid of the water and doesn't like to get her face wet in the pool. Her mom really wants her to learn to swim so Marie can help her watch her little brother in the backyard pool and so Marie can have fun in the summer with her friends.

Marie started her swimming lessons at the YWCA last week and she doesn't like them one bit. The water's too cold and she can't float like the other kids. She wants her mom to take her out of the classes. Her mom says, "Absolutely not."

The Problem: _____

_____

The Facts: _____

_____

_____

_____

Weigh the alternatives:	What makes you think this is a good solution (the pluses)?	What would happen if your solution was wrong (the minuses)?
Alternative A		
Alternative B		
Alternative C		

Write down the best solution you can. _____

_____

_____

_____

Act on the solution and make changes in the solution if necessary. _____

_____

_____

CASE #37: THE CASE OF THE MATH PROBLEM

When Wayne started having a problem with math in school, he wasn't sure what to do. All his friends are in honors classes and know math really well, but he felt weird asking them for help. He didn't think it was cool to ask your friends for help.

Wayne's teacher approached him last week and said that if he didn't get a tutor for math, he may fail it for the year and be held back. Wayne's friend Mark is an after-school math tutor, but he's still afraid Mark might make fun of him.

The Problem: _____

_____

The Facts: _____

_____

_____

_____

_____

Weigh the alternatives:	What makes you think this is a good solution (the pluses)?	What would happen if your solution was wrong (the minuses)?
Alternative A		
Alternative B		
Alternative C		

Write down the best solution you can. _____

_____

_____

_____

Act on the solution and make changes in the solution if necessary. _____

_____

_____

_____

CASE #38: THE CASE OF THE SPOILED BIKE RIDER

Terry really wants a bike. All her friends have them, but Terry's mom doesn't think she'll appreciate it if it's just given to her. Terry got the skates she wanted for her birthday but then never even used them.

Her mom's solution is for Terry to do chores around the house to earn money towards the bike, and when she earns enough for half, her mom will pay for the other half. None of Terry's friends have to do chores after school, but they all have bikes to ride in the annual bike race which is in two months. She doesn't think she could earn enough in two months. Terry wishes her parents would just give her the bike so she could ride in the race, and then she'd do the chores later.

The Problem: _____

_____

The Facts: _____

_____

_____

_____

_____

Weigh the alternatives:	What makes you think this is a good solution (the pluses)?	What would happen if your solution was wrong (the minuses)?
Alternative A		
Alternative B		
Alternative C		

Write down the best solution you can. _____

_____

_____

_____

Act on the solution and make changes in the solution if necessary. _____

_____

_____

CASE #39: THE CASE OF THE LATE SLEEPER

Sam just doesn't get why his parents won't let him stay up as late as they do. Whenever they watch a movie on TV, he never gets to see the end because he has to go to bed at 8:30. Just once he'd like to stay up as late as his older brother. He's never even tired when he goes to bed and usually lays there staring at the ceiling for a half hour before he even falls asleep.

In the mornings though, Sam's mom can barely get him up to eat breakfast. He just crawls back under the covers. His teacher has even called his mom saying Sam's eyes are really heavy in class and he doesn't pay much attention until around third period.

The Problem: _____
_____

The Facts: _____
_____
_____
_____
_____

Weigh the alternatives:	What makes you think this is a good solution (the pluses)?	What would happen if your solution was wrong (the minuses)?
Alternative A		
Alternative B		
Alternative C		

Write down the best solution you can. _____
_____
_____
_____

Act on the solution and make changes in the solution if necessary. _____
_____
_____
_____

CASE #40: THE CASE OF THE UNEATEN VEGETABLES

Tina refuses to eat her vegetables at dinner. Her mom has tried to make all different kinds for her to try, but Tina says they all taste awful. She feeds them to her dog under the table when her parents aren't looking.

Lately, Tina has been feeling really tired, too tired to play tag at recess. All she wants to do is watch TV after school. Her mom took her to the doctor to find out what was wrong, and the doctor said Tina's not getting enough vitamins like the ones you get from broccoli or peas or peppers. He suggested she eat more vegetables.

The Problem: _____

The Facts: _____
_____
_____
_____
_____

Weigh the alternatives:	What makes you think this is a good solution (the pluses)?	What would happen if your solution was wrong (the minuses)?
Alternative A		
Alternative B		
Alternative C		

Write down the best solution you can. _____
_____
_____

Act on the solution and make changes in the solution if necessary. _____
_____
_____

This is to certify that

is a Master Detective and Problem-Solver

Signed _____